bad dogs!

THOMAS DUNNE BOOKS.

An imprint of St. Martin's Press.

www.thomasdunnebooks.com

www.stmartins.com

The Library of Congress Cataloging-in-Publication Data is available upon request

ISBN 978-1-250-10499-1 (paper over board)

ISBN 978-1-250-10500-4 (e-book)

St. Martin's Press books may be purchased for educational, business, or promotional use. For
information on bulk purchases, please contact the Macmillan Corporate and Premium Sales
Department at 1-800-221-7945, extension 5442, or write to specialmarkets@macmillan.com

First published in the United Kingdom by Virgin Books, an imprint of Ebury Publishing

First Edition: September 2015

First U.S. Edition: October 2016

10 9 8 7 6 5 4 3 2 1

bad dogs!

Thomas Dunne Books

St. Martin's Griffin

New York

BOOZE HOUND

SWAMP THING

DOG WASHER

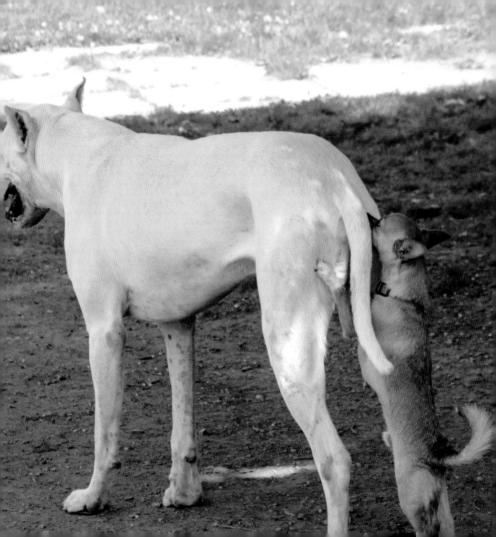

BEST SEAT IN THE HOUSE

BBQ TIME!

WALKIES

FETCH!

BALLS

WHO LET THE DOGS OUT?

THIRSTY WORK

HOT DOG

DOG-EARED

MAIL RETRIEVER

DOG POUND

TERRIERFIED

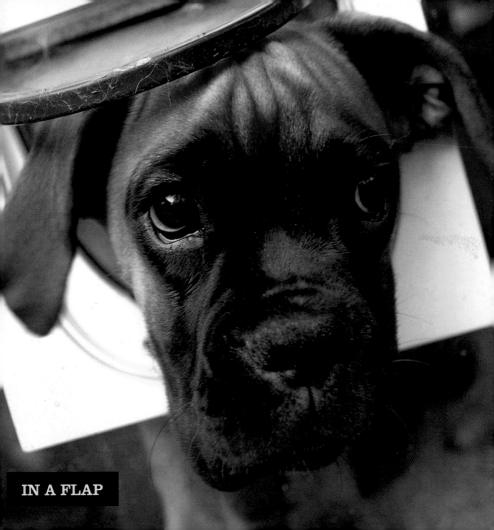

IN A FLAP

LAZY BOY

FOOD COMA

BURIED TREASURE

DON'T BITE MY HEAD OFF

BATH TIME

PIE LIKE THAT

TIGHT SPOT

KITCHEN RAIDERS

THE GREAT ESCAPE

MISBEEHAVING

IN HOT WATER

LOVE AT FIRST SNIFF

HOUSE-TRAINED

IMPUGSONATOR

OVER INDULGED

FRIDGE RAIDERS

HAPPY ENDINGS

BFF

THE DOG ATE IT...

DOG MARLEY

WASN'T ME

HIDE AND SEEK

Picture Credits

Pg 4. Sherlock – Steve Hall
Pg 5. Shutterstock
Pg 6. Barney – Meg Price
Pg 7. Deborah McClinton / Getty Images
Pg 8. James A. Guilliam / Getty Images
Pg 9. Butch Martin / Getty Images
Pg 10. Arthur Tilley / Getty Images
Pg 11. Harley – Trish Aleve www.pawsomepetphotography.com
Pg 12. Cadence – Aaron McCollough
Pg 13. Mesa – Julie Steiner
Pg 14. iStock / Getty Images
Pg 15. Window Washers – Michael J Klokow
Pg 16. Debra Bardowicks / Getty Images
Pg 17. Terry J. Alcom / Getty Images
Pg 18. Buster – Trish Aleve www.pawsomepetphotography.com
Pg 19. Moose – Julie Steiner
Pg 20. Leila Cutler / Alamy
Pg 21. Romeo rides Rubin – Patii www.facebook.com/patiigraphy
Pg 22. iStock / Getty Images
Pg 23. Shutterstock
Pg 24. iStock / Getty Images
Pg 25. iStock / Getty Images
Pg 26. Shutterstock
Pg 27. iStock / Getty Images
Pg 28. Pip and Milo – Stuart Graham
Pg 29. George – Heather West
Pg 30. Shutterstock
Pg 31. PM Images / Getty Images
Pg 32. Heidi – Scott Cromwell www.scottcromwellphoto.com
Pg 33. Angel and Eve – Steve Hall
Pg 34. Shutterstock
Pg 35. Diane Diederich / Getty Images
Pg 36. Halo –Steve Hall
Pg 37. Winston – Scott Cromwell www.scottcromwellphoto.com
Pg 38. Mr.Bean – K. Reifman
Pg 39. Shutterstock
Pg 40. Gandee Vasan / Getty Images
Pg 41. Justin Paget / Corbis

Pg 42. Gandee Vasan /Getty Images
Pg 43. Halo – Steve Hall
Pg 44. Shutterstock
Pg 45. Emma the Boxer – Morten Skogaard
Pg 46. Rumi – Jim Girardi
Pg 47. Cruise – Mike Frighetto
Pg 48. Bandit – Gerald Brazell
Pg 49. Photos 12 / Alamy
Pg 50. Stephen Swintek / Getty Images
Pg 51. Juniors Bildarchiv GmbH / Alamy
Pg 52. Enli – Sarita Dawn
Pg 53. Chuck Hopkins
Pg 54. Shutterstock
Pg 55. Urban Dog – Fleur – Ange Lamothe
Pg 56. Color Blind / Getty Images
Pg 57. Blickwinkel / Alamy
Pg 58. Casper – Marley Adams
Pg 59. iStock / Getty Images
Pg 60. Trixie – Emery Way
Pg 61. Hollywood Buster Harley – Trish Aleve www.pawsomepetphotography.com
Pg 62. Shiba Dogs – HsinChen Shih
Pg 63. Mesa and Moose – Julie Steiner
Pg 64. Shutterstock
Pg 65. Shutterstock
Pg 66. Mesa – Julie Steiner
Pg 67. Bert – Pete Aighton
Pg 68. Harley – Trish Aleve www.pawsomepetphotography.com
Pg 69. Moose –Julie Steiner
Pg 70. Tika and Harley – Trish Aleve www.pawsomepetphotography.com
Pg 71. Hollywood – Trish Aleve www.pawsomepetphotography.com
Pg 72. Darren Boucher / Getty Images
Pg 73. David Mendelsohn/Masterfile/ Corbis
Pg 74. Corona and Bailey – Tina Moreau
Pg 75. Shutterstock
Pg 76. iStock / Getty Images
Pg 77. Bailey – Dave Webster
Pg 78. Jay P. Morgan / Getty Images

Pg 79. John Terrence Turner / Getty Images
Pg 80. Debra Bardowicks / Getty Images
Pg 81. Barney – Meg Price
Pg 82. iStock / Getty Images
Pg 83. iStock / Getty Images
Pg 84. Buster and Harley – Trish Aleve www.pawsomepetphotography.com
Pg 85. Int Ch & Multi Ch Chesapeake's Cruzin to the Top ("Journey") – Yanvarina Robbins
Pg 86. Buster – Trish Aleve www.pawsomepetphotography.com
Pg 87. Shutterstock
Pg 88. Heidi – Scott Cromwell www.scottcromwellphoto.com
Pg 89. Shutterstock
Pg 90. Trixie – Emery Way
Pg 91. Moose – Julie Steiner
Pg 92. Back in the Pack / Getty Images
Pg 93. iStock / Getty Images
Pg 94. Bailey – Dave Webster
Pg 95. Melanie Acevedo / Getty Images
Pg 96. PM Images / Getty Images
Pg 97. Patrick Brooks Brandenburg / Getty Images
Pg 98. Yoshi and Sasha – Natalie
Pg 99. Barney and Dilly – Meg Price
Pg 100. Leah – Malc Smith
Pg 101. Thomas Jackson / Getty Images
Pg 102. Martin Poole / Getty Images
Pg 103. Ian Payne / Getty Images
Pg 104 Sartore Joel / Getty Images
Pg 105. Tango – Richard Hurley
Pg 106. Marlo Parnell / Getty Images
Pg 107. Niko – Lina Custodio
Pg 108. Shutterstock
Pg 109. Karen and Ian Stewart / Alamy
Pg 110. Shutterstock
Pg 111. Shutterstock